WHAT WOULD
JESUS
POST?

WHAT WOULD JESUS POST?

SEVEN PRINCIPLES
CHRISTIANS SHOULD FOLLOW IN SOCIAL MEDIA

BRIAN D. WASSOM

WestBow
PRESS
A DIVISION OF THOMAS NELSON

WestBow Press books may be ordered through booksellers or by contacting:

WestBow Press
A Division of Thomas Nelson
1663 Liberty Drive
Bloomington, IN 47403
www.westbowpress.com
1 (866) 928-1240

Because of the dynamic nature of the Internet, any web addresses or
links contained in this book may have changed since publication and
may no longer be valid. The views expressed in this work are solely those
of the author and do not necessarily reflect the views of the publisher,
and the publisher hereby disclaims any responsibility for them.

Certain stock imagery © Thinkstock.
Any people depicted in stock imagery provided by Thinkstock are
models, and such images are being used for illustrative purposes only.

Unless otherwise noted, all Biblical quotations in this book are taken from
the Holy Bible, New Living Translation, copyright ©1996, 2004, 2007
by Tyndale House Foundation. Used by permission of Tyndale House
Publishers, Inc., Carol Stream, Illinois 60188. All rights reserved.

Quotations marked (NIV) are from THE HOLY BIBLE, NEW
INTERNATIONAL VERSION®, NIV® Copyright © 1973, 1978, 1984, 2011
by Biblica, Inc.® and are used by permission. All rights reserved worldwide.

Quotations marked (ESV) are from The Holy Bible, English Standard
Version® (ESV®), copyright © 2001 by Crossway, a publishing ministry
of Good News Publishers. Used by permission. All rights reserved.

ISBN: 978-1-4908-1163-5 (e)
ISBN: 978-1-4908-1162-8 (sc)
ISBN: 978-1-4908-1164-2 (hc)

Library of Congress Control Number: 2013918431

Printed in the United States of America.

WestBow Press rev. date: 10/25/2013

Acknowledgements and Dedication

This book would never have materialized without the encouragement and insights of the pastors and elders of my faith family, Rockpointe Community Church. Many of the thoughts developed here originated during conversations on how to best guide our congregation through the spiritual challenges of an always-on digital world.

Nor would I have seen this project through to completion without the emotional and editorial support of my wife, Sheri, who makes each of my days better by being in it. Special thanks as well to Mickey Badalamenti for helpful feedback on text and design.

I dedicate this book to Eva and Dayton, for whom today's media will be a quaint relic by the time they reach adulthood. May this text be only one of many influences leading them along the path of Biblical wisdom for the rest of their days.

Table of Contents

Introduction

"With great power comes great responsibility."

If the *Spiderman* movies have done nothing else, they have certainly ingrained that particular phrase into the public consciousness. But Jesus told us something very similar two thousand years ago. In Luke 12:48, he says, "When someone has been given much, much will be required in return; and when someone has been entrusted with much, even more will be required." In other words, when God gives us the power to make a difference in the lives of others, He expects us to *use* that power, and to use it *well*.

And make no mistake: social media gives us great power indeed. As a society, we've already become so accustomed to the internet that we rarely stop to appreciate what a revolutionary achievement it is.

Never before has virtually every person on the planet had an opportunity to communicate with every other person, let alone in real time, through text, images and video. Book publishing, recorded music, filmmaking, news reporting, banking, and retail are just a few of the industries that have been radically transformed or nearly eliminated by this advance in communications technology. It is only relatively recently that the technology became ubiquitous and mobile enough to insert itself into our daily social lives and interactions with friends. But in a few short years it has already reshaped the way we engage in even those basic activities every bit as much as it has reshaped the way we shop for books or music. That is a level of power that the greatest kings and most successful despots in human history could scarcely have dreamed of wielding.

That is why I believe it is vitally important for we who identify as Christ-followers to pay attention to social media. If we take seriously Jesus' command in Matthew 22:37-40 to "love the Lord your God with all your heart and with all your soul and with all your mind … [and] love your neighbor as yourself," and if we recognize the power that social media can have both on our own hearts and minds and on our relationships with others, then we need to be asking ourselves such questions as, "Am I honoring God with how I use social media?" "What effect are these sites having on me as a person?" and "How could I use this technology to be a better friend to the people in my life?"

I wrote this book because I couldn't find another one that was asking these questions or suggesting answers from a Biblical viewpoint. The need for these types of conversations is abundant. In my professional life, I spend a lot of time both litigating commercial disputes and writing legal commentary. In both contexts, I constantly encounter new examples of how people misbehave in social media, and how they allow themselves to say and do things online that they likely would have never done in another context. Likewise, in the leadership role I hold within my church community, I have seen far too much evidence of social media's corrosive effects on the lives of those around me. Loose words and poorly thought-out actions online have ruined relationships, caused offense, and even soured people on faith altogether.

Yet despite all of this fallout, I've also seen much good come out of interactions that took place, in whole or in part, online. People have been drawn back into fellowship by their Facebook friends. Others have delivered encouragement to people in times of need that they wouldn't have known about if not for social media. But social media itself is morally neutral. The ability to interact with others online is a tool, nothing more. Whether it affects people for good or for ill depends entirely on how we choose to use it.

One thing, however, is certain: social media is not going away. The names and capabilities of the particular services we use will inevitably change, sometimes at a very rapid pace. But the internet itself exists as a means for communication. Its utility has broadened over the years from its original military purpose to commercial and ultimately social communication, in part because we humans have a fundamental need to interact with other people. It is safe to say, therefore, that our communications technology will never get less social than it already is. Studies show that as many as 98% of Americans between the ages of 18-24 already use at least one social media site. Over a billion people—about a seventh of the world's population—have Facebook accounts, and the average amount of time that a Facebook user spends on the site is more than 15 hours every month. Like it or not, online communication is destined to be a vital component of how people across the world interact with each other for the foreseeable future.

How, then, should we live in that online space? What does it mean to love God and love others in social media? The following is my attempt to answer those questions from a Biblical perspective. I've broken the discussion down into seven basic principles that I believe are important for all Christians to keep in mind as they interact online.

Seven Principles
for Using Social Media

Think before you *post*

"What's on your mind?"

That's what Facebook asks as soon as we log in. Other social media sites encourage us to share what we're doing, to comment on something a friend said, or the review the meal we're eating—all the things we'd probably talk about with our friends if they were right there with us. In fact, that's exactly how the companies behind these sites want us to think of social media—as just another way to make spontaneous, informal, and unfiltered chit-chat with friends.

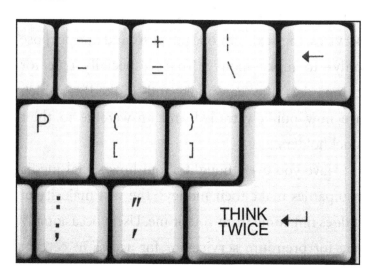

The one thing they *don't* encourage us to do is to think twice before we post, because that sort of restraint might result in us sharing less information about ourselves online.

We get very different instructions from the Bible. Proverbs 15:28 says, "The heart of the godly *thinks carefully before speaking*," while Proverbs 17:27 (NIV) observes, "one who has knowledge uses words with restraint."

To understand the difference between how social media companies and the Bible would have us behave, consider the motivations of each. Social media companies are no more evil or untrustworthy than any other group of human beings. But like any company, regardless of whatever interesting conversation or social good may come from their services, they exist for one purpose, and one purpose only—to make money. That's especially true for companies like Facebook and LinkedIn, which are now publicly traded and answerable to their stockholders.

Have you ever thought about how social media companies make their money? The vast majority of it does not come from you or me. Users occasionally pay for premium services or for access to certain games, but by and large, it's free to create an account and free to interact with our friends on social media sites. And yet these companies make money, hand over fist.

There's a saying that has been around for a while and become particularly apt with regard to social media: "if you're not paying for it, then you're not the customer—you're the product." Social media companies make money by gathering, and selling access to, as much information about us as possible. All those disparate bits of information we share online are generally innocuous in and of themselves, but when gathered into a central database, they add up to form a huge repository of information about us as potential customers.

Advertisers salivate over that information. Why run an advertisement in relatively dumb print or broadcast media when you can target your message to the exact demographic categories most likely to respond to it? The more unique, broad, detailed, and robust a social media site's database of user information is, the higher of a price the company can charge advertisers for access to it.

Missing from that equation is any consideration of the consequences sharing the information might have on the lives of those who share it. That's our responsibility, not theirs. Again, social media companies aren't morally evil for wanting our information. This is their business, pure and simple.

Speaking well

The Bible, on the other hand, is concerned with making us right with—and more like—God in all aspects of our lives. The Book of Proverbs (in verses 1:3-4, NIV) is very clear about its purpose. It exists:

> For gaining wisdom …;
>
> for receiving instruction in prudent behavior,
>
> doing what is right and just and fair; for giving prudence to those who are simple,
>
> knowledge and discretion to the young.

Wisdom has been called "skill in the art of Godly living." And one critical element of that skill, as we've seen, is thinking carefully before we speak.

That's because there are real and severe consequences to speaking foolishly. "Where words are many," says Proverbs 10:19 (NIV), "sin is not absent," and "those who love to talk will reap the consequences," according to Proverbs 18:21. Jesus himself warned in Matthew 12:36-37 (ESV) that our foolish words will not go unnoticed, or unpunished:

> I tell you, on the day of judgment you will have to give an account for every careless word you speak; for by your words you will be justified, and by your words you will be condemned.

Our friends might not catch everything we share online, but God doesn't miss a thing.

Being slow to speak not only helps us avoid saying stupid things, it also gives our words more force when we say the *right* things. And pausing to consider the effect of our words will help us discern the right time to speak. Foolish words bring harm, but words used well can "bring life," says Proverbs 18:21. Proverbs 25:11 says, "Timely advice is lovely, like golden apples in a silver basket." A sharpshooter takes time to focus and aim so that his bullet hits the target instead of being wasted and potentially causing unintended harm. Similarly, we should use the powerful arsenal of words at our disposal sparingly, so as to cause the maximum amount of good and avoid collateral damage.

I listed this principle first for a reason. Although there are several considerations to keep in mind for using social media well, none of the rest of them matter if you aren't paying attention to what you say.

To your *own self* be true

The Temptation to Role-Play

Just as it's important to be mindful of what you *say* online, so too is it vital to remember who you *are*. The internet offers a near-perfect opportunity to become someone else, or to be completely anonymous. This is not an inherently bad thing. One of the first things we learn to do as children is to role-play (a hobby that gamer geeks like me never completely abandon). Sometimes the only way to gain empathy for another is to "walk a mile in their shoes," as the saying goes. And anonymous speech has had a cherished role in our democratic system at least since the pre-Revolutionary War pamphlets of Thomas Paine.

But more often than not, anonymity and role-playing in social media are neither innocent nor noble. Without a verifiable identity, we lack accountability. And when we are not accountable to others, the social norms that keep us polite and considerate in face-to-face conversation break down just as quickly as they did in the literary classic *Lord of the Flies*. For evidence, just look at the comment sections that follow almost any online news article. Rather than thoughtful insight into the issue at hand, these comments usually contain nothing but vitriol, political grandstanding and name-calling. What for most publishers began as a grand experiment in audience engagement has become an embarrassment.[1] Many publications now hide the comment sections in areas where they aren't immediately visible to most readers, or have eliminated them altogether.

Creating new online profiles for ourselves on various social media sites can be a bit like attending a new school or moving to a new town—an opportunity to reinvent ourselves. To start from scratch in creating the persona we want others to see. This is especially true when we tailor our profiles to fit the ethos of a particular site. For example, LinkedIn is geared toward business professionals, so I'm unlikely to post pictures there from my night out with friends, or share status updates about a new restaurant I tried. The ethos of Facebook, on the other hand, is precisely the opposite; I feel awkward sharing too much about my professional life there. Even if I'm not trying to be someone I'm not when I post to one of these sites, I certainly feel like I'm wearing a different hat depending on which site it is.

The danger here is the temptation to compartmentalize our lives, to the point that the way we behave and hold ourselves out in one context is not only different from, but incompatible with, how we act in another context. Put simply: we become hypocrites.

To be sure, social media is not the only place where this happens. Anyone who has attended a church for any length of time—and many who haven't—have wondered just how authentic the glowing faces of many Christians around them really are. And far too many of us justify that cynicism by not following the same moral guidelines from Monday to Saturday that we espouse on Sundays.

Raising the stakes

Social media can magnify the consequences of hypocrisy in at least a couple important ways. First, it creates a permanent record. It's bad enough to use foul language, drink too much, or gossip about someone at the bar on a Friday night. It's worse when we leave evidence of it online, where it will never be forgotten.

Second, the audience is much broader. As a result, the impact that our mistakes can have on our reputations is far more severe. Verse 10:1 in the Book of Ecclesiastes—another deep well of Biblical wisdom—warns: "As dead flies cause even a bottle of perfume to stink, so a little foolishness spoils great wisdom and honor." This wise advice has been repeated throughout human history. Benjamin Franklin said it this way: "It takes many good deeds to build a good reputation, and only one bad one to lose it."

In a world where our offhand comments are only heard by those around us, these warnings could be read somewhat figuratively. Applied to social media, however, they are quite literal. Take the example of Scott Bartosiewicz. In March 2011, he was a 28-year-old up-and-comer in the field of digital marketing. The agency he worked for counted major brands like Chrysler as its clients.

One day, Scott found himself late for a meeting because he was stuck in traffic on a Detroit-area highway—not an uncommon occurrence for those in this area. With no other way to vent his frustration, he pulled out his phone and sent this message via Twitter:

> "I find it ironic that Detroit is known as the motor city and yet no one here knows how to … drive."

You probably could have heard this sort of grousing coming out of the mouths of many drivers around Scott that day. More than likely, some of them even shared it online. But what Scott failed to realize was that his phone was not logged in to his personal Twitter account; instead, it was opened to @ChryslerAutos, the official Twitter account of his client, Chrysler. Instantly, his fleeting gripe was transmitted to hundreds of thousands of Chrysler's followers as an official communication of the company. From there, the post instantly went viral around the world.

To no one's surprise, Scott was fired that day. But the pain multiplied days later when Chrysler chose not to renew its contract with Scott's employer. That probably meant that several of Scott's co-workers lost their jobs as well.

Scott's professional life is not over; he has been able to find work again. But his career path is certainly different as a result of that one mistake. For the rest of his life, his name and photo will be associated with this story online. And Scott's experience is not unique; a week rarely goes by without a similar online gaffe finding its way into the news.

This matters because our reputation is one of the most valuable things we possess. Proverbs 22:1 (NIV) says, "A good name is more desirable than great riches; to be esteemed is better than silver or gold." And in Shakespeare's play *Othello*, one character says, "Good name in man and woman . . . [i]s the immediate jewel of their souls." Another character in the same play whose reputation becomes ruined laments, "I have lost the immortal part of myself, and what remains is bestial."

For Christians, the pain of a tarnished reputation is even worse, because we have been commissioned to convey a message that goes beyond ourselves: the truth of the Gospel. When we allow our reputations to be tarnished, we also soil our message.

But there is opportunity here as well. The internet's way of mashing up the different compartments of our lives on one globally accessible network can offer Christians new avenues for sharing their faith. A professional acquaintance who connects with you on LinkedIn may find out more about your social life by looking you up on Facebook as well, and vice-versa. And when one or more of our online profiles include our Christian testimony, they can break the ice on that conversation in ways we may not have pursued otherwise. Indeed, being aware of social media's power to hold us accountable should encourage us to be more bold in making our faith visible, and our behavior consistent, in every facet of our lives. It takes away our excuses and our hiding places.

You only get one hat online. Make sure it's one you want to be seen wearing.

Guard your heart

What's at stake

Anyone who has spent any significant amount of time in the church is bound to be familiar with Proverbs 4:23's injunction, "Guard your heart." Far fewer of us, however, fully appreciate what this means. Too often it's reduced to ancient dating advice for teenaged girls. That application is valid, of course, but the verse means so much more.

First, it's important to recall that ancient Israelites did not have the separate concepts of "heart" and "mind" as we do today. Rather, the Hebrew word we translate as "heart" means our entire inner selves—emotion, intellect, and will. Proverbs 27:19 reflects this concept when it says, "As a face is reflected in water, so the heart reflects the real person." This verse also reminds us that this inner person—not the one we hold ourselves out to be in public—is who we *really* are. That's where God looks in order to assess our righteousness; as Proverbs 17:3 says, "the Lord tests the heart." This helps explain why our hearts—our true selves—are such important objects for scrutiny.

What does it mean, then, to "guard" our hearts? A guard is a gatekeeper. He stands in the gap between what he protects and everything else. Only if something is worthy of entrance and poses no threat to those inside will he let it in. That is the attitude we are to take towards our own "hearts"—our own inner selves. We should carefully evaluate every behavior, experience, and thought pattern we engage in, and determine whether the influence it has on our thoughts, feelings, choices, and beliefs is beneficial or harmful. Paul echoes this idea in 2 Corinthians 10:5 (NIV) when he implores believers to "take captive every thought and make it obedient to Christ."

But how do we do that? Reading the familiar proverb in context (together with verses 23-27) suggests an answer:

> Guard your heart above all else,
>
> for it determines the course of your life.
>
> Avoid all perverse talk; stay away from corrupt speech.
>
> Look straight ahead, and fix your eyes on what lies before you.
>
> Mark out a straight path for your feet;
>
> stay on the safe path.

Don't get sidetracked;

keep your feet from following evil.

Our hearts are conditioned by our behavior. To avoid corrupting ourselves, therefore, this passage warns us to not speak evil words, to keep our minds off evil subjects, and to avoid doing evil things.

It's more than merely our reputations that are stake—it's our very selves. The famous American novelist Kurt Vonnegut put it best: "We are what we pretend to be, so we must be careful about what we pretend to be."[2] The values and aspirations upon which we focus our attention reveal what is truly inside us. We may be drawn to think and behave in a certain way online that we would have never done anywhere else. But if we nurture that second life to the point that it becomes what we truly desire, the role becomes our true self, both inside and out.

We see the effect of this phenomenon in the countless marriages that have been ruined by what began as role-playing through social media. I've known at least one person—and read about many more—whose infidelity began merely as an online fantasy, but grew until it became very much real. And Jesus called out the false distinction between virtual and physical cheating in Matthew 5:28 when he warned men that "anyone who even looks at a woman with lust has already committed adultery with her in his heart." In some jurisdictions today, as many as one in three divorce cases now cite a spouse's communications on Facebook as a component of what broke up the relationship.

But this truth of human nature runs both ways. Focusing our attention on the people and things we want to emulate will naturally cause us to become more like them. British songwriter Vicky Beeching turned this into a plea to God in her song "Captivated":

> Beholding is becoming, so as You fill my gaze
>
> I become more like You and my heart is changed
>
> Beholding is becoming, so as You fill my view
>
> Transform me into the likeness of You

Perhaps this is why Paul exhorts us in Philippians 4:8 to "[f]ix your thoughts on what is true, and honorable, and right, and pure, and lovely, and admirable. Think about things that are excellent and worthy of praise." Today, he would give the same advice about the pages we "like" and the comments we post.

With this in mind, let's think about what it means to "guard your heart" while using social media.

Shaping our desires

The things on which we fix our gazes don't need to be outwardly dark or evil to be a bad influence on our hearts. Indeed, some of the most difficult influences to overcome are the ones we find most appealing. We live in a culture that knows this truth very well—and profits handsomely from it. Fully 70% of the United States' gross domestic product consists of consumer spending. So the companies that sell us those goods and services have an existential stake in us buying more.

In order to get us to buy more, these retailers first need to get us to *want* more. Fortunately for them, it's not difficult. Desire for personal gratification seems to be hard-wired into the human heart. Often, all you need to do to get someone to want a thing is to show them that it exists. Once that happens, the previously satisfactory status quo just won't seem good enough anymore.

This is a truth we've long understood. Way back in 1919, vaudeville artist Nora Bayes captured it in the chorus of her smash hit "How Ya Gonna Keep 'Em Down on the Farm?":

How ya gonna keep 'em down on the farm

After they've seen Paree'

How ya gonna keep 'em away from Broadway

Jazzin around and paintin' the town

How ya gonna keep 'em away from harm, that's a mystery

They'll never want to see a rake or plow

And who the deuce can parleyvous a cow?

How ya gonna keep 'em down on the farm

After they've seen Paree'

Bayes' song was inspired by the new European perspectives that American farm boys had gained after fighting for the French in World War I. But it could just as well have described the experience that millions have every day using social media.

Nowhere, in my experience, is this more true than on Pinterest. This site rose from obscurity to become the third-most popular social media site in the country by performing one very specific function—being what I call "the catalog of all that which is cute." Pinterest's users (about 90% of whom are female) collect, share, and spend a lot of time viewing images of things they find visually appealing or emotionally satisfying. Of course, this is by no means an inherently bad thing. I've lost count of how many useful, crafty ideas I've seen implemented by someone who said, "I found that on Pinterest."

But even if we have no intention of acquiring every desirable thing we see online—and how could we?—the act of constantly fueling our desires has consequences for our inner peace. Before we realize it, our own worlds can come to seem exceedingly small, and our own possessions woefully inadequate.

This phenomenon extends beyond the things we own. I've spoken to several people, Christians and otherwise, that find themselves disenchanted after reading one too many "happy" status updates on Facebook. Seeing your cute kids, healthy relationships, and fun vacations isn't always encouraging to those who don't have their own. And in response, many people often feel pressure (whether subtle or overt) to make the content they share online a little rosier than their lives actually are. For the discontented, social media can provide a never-ending list of Joneses to keep up with.

As understandable as these feelings are, though, they're also a sin. Like, a big one. Ask anyone on the street what they think God's basic rules for life are, and more likely than not, they'll cite the Ten Commandments. Yet far fewer people remember that coveting—*i.e.*, desiring to possess something that someone else has—is one of the things prohibited by that fundamental code.

In Exodus 20:17, God gave the Tenth Commandment: "You must not covet your neighbor's house. You must not covet your neighbor's wife, male or female servant, ox or donkey, or anything else that belongs to your neighbor." Desire itself isn't prohibited, but rather wanting something that doesn't belong to you. Applying this verse in a post-industrial, consumer economy takes some thought. At the time Moses carried these commandments down from Mt. Sinai, the Israelites couldn't go to Costco or Amazon and order a duplicate of something their neighbor owned. They had to take it away from the neighbor in order to get it. So it's not necessarily wrong to want the same model of car or style of house that your friend owns. But it is wrong to want his or her *actual* car or house—or, if we apply the spirit of the commandment faithfully—to want something just *because* your friend owns something like it. (Of course, the *people* in our friends' households are no more fungible today than they ever were, and the lusts we feel for them are just as big of a problem now as they were in Moses' day.)

The Tenth Commandment was hard enough to follow in Moses' time, when the only "neighbors" most people encountered were the ones walking alongside them in the desert. Social media magnifies the temptation to covet—and, hence, the commandment's importance—by showing us the things and relationships possessed by hundreds, if not thousands, of people on a daily basis. It is basic human nature for our desires to be stimulated by at least some of those things we see, just as it is our fundamental duty as Christ-followers to keep ourselves from indulging in those impulses. And to the extent that becomes a problem for us online, the prudent course for guarding our hearts from those desires is to limit or avoid contact with the sites that stir them up.

One final thought on this point. Be careful of turning Paul's advice to think about things that are "beautiful," "excellent" or "praiseworthy" into an excuse for covetousness or lust. By definition, the objects of our desires are things we find "beautiful" or "excellent." But Paul's instruction isn't a license to want such things; it is a warning not to dwell on sinful thoughts. This is an example of why it's important to read and interpret the Scriptures in context, rather than in isolation.

Reprogramming our thoughts

"Walk with the wise and become wise; associate with fools and get in trouble," says Proverbs 13:20. As with many proverbs—being, as they are, poetry— applying this one is as much about the spirit of the verse as it is the literal language. Rarely do we ever encounter someone we'd label as entirely "wise" or "foolish." That said, with a little wisdom, we can discern which companions are good influences on our behavior, and which ones aren't. And the latter are the ones we need to guard our hearts against.

In C. S. Lewis' classic study of human relationships *The Four Loves*, he explains the subtle but profound power that friends hold over our thoughts and opinions. "Alone among unsympathetic companions," he writes, "I hold certain views and standards timidly, half ashamed to avow them and half doubtful if they can after all be right. Put me back among my Friends and in [ten minutes,] these same views and standards become once more indisputable." The reason is that our friends are the persons whose opinions we care about. Whether subtly or consciously, it is their approval we seek. So long as the people we care about and respect are on the same page as us, we care little about what anyone else thinks.

And since we use "friend" and similar terms to describe the people we associate with through social media, it should be no surprise that we see this phenomenon play out openly online. Facebook clued into this years ago when it introduced social advertising. No matter how targeted a retailer's advertisement is to our particular likes and desires, we will always perceive it as an advertisement, and hence it will only have so much influence on us. But what Facebook discovered is that merely letting someone know what their online friends "like" or are doing is far more likely to get users' attention than any direct advertisement. Again, that's because it's our friends' opinions that truly carry weight with us.

The popularity of online "memes" over the last few years, however, shows that more than just marketers understand this truth and are using it to their benefit. What most people nowadays refer to as "memes" consist of a single image with text superimposed at the top and bottom. These taglines are very akin to the proverbs themselves—pithy couplets meant to drive home a single point. They've become especially popular with teens and those who want to make a political or religious point in a particularly witty or sarcastic way. "Meme" is also used to describe such internet-fueled fads as "planking" photos and "Harlem Shake" videos.

It's the political and religious messaging, though, that is most true to the original intent of the term. The proper definition of "meme" is "an idea, behavior, or style that spreads from person to person within a culture." It was coined in 1976 by Richard Dawkins, an evolutionary biologist who is very vocal about his social agenda to militantly promote atheism and attack religious belief. As one of the most visible figures in the New Atheism movement, Dawkins— whose signature book is *The God Delusion*—considers religious faith one of the world's "great evils."[3]

The "meme" concept was Dawkins' attempt to translate the precepts of biological evolutionary theory to human culture. Evolutionary thought holds that certain genes pass from generation to generation, with some adapting and mutating to grow stronger and more complex, while others proving less useful and dying out. Dawkins suggested that ideas and cultural norms (*i.e.*, "memes") behave in much the same way.

The most dangerous falsehoods are the ones that contain an element of truth. Memetic theory has surface-level appeal, because one must admit that "catchy" ideas like pop songs and advertising slogans *can* exhibit some of the characteristics that Dawkins describes. And as I've mentioned repeatedly here, both the Bible and our own experiences confirm the profound effect that various subconscious influences can have on our thoughts and beliefs.

But Dawkins betrays his personal motivations and undermines the credibility of his theory when he applies the meme concept to religion. In *The Selfish Gene*, the same 1976 book in which he coined the term "meme," Dawkins confessed: "As an enthusiastic Darwinian, I have been dissatisfied with explanations that my fellow-enthusiasts have offered for human behaviour. They have tried to look for 'biological advantages' in various attributes of human civilization ... [such as] religion[.]"[4] In a materialistic, evolutionary worldview, biologic advantage is the sole explanation for everything. Because he was forced to admit that religion did not bestow any such biological edge on its adherents, Dawkins did not have a tidy means for explaining away religious behavior. That is, until he invented the concept of "memes" as a mechanism for importing an evolutionary worldview into human behavior without needing to involve biology at all.

Dawkins' followers carried the ball further for him on this issue. They have labeled "religious memes"—especially those of Christianity, wrote Aaron Lynch in the ominously-titled book *Thought Contagion*—as especially powerful, and developed all manner of theories to explain their persistence.

Of course, none of these explanations have been concerned with whether or not the ideas themselves were actually *true*. To the contrary, memetic theory allows these authors to treat all cultural ideas, religious or otherwise, as mere objects that behave in defined and predictable ways.

And of course, when something can be quantified and predicted, it can (at least theoretically) be controlled and manipulated. Hence the term "memetic engineering," which is very much what it sounds like: think genetic engineering, but with human culture instead of body chemistry. It is the attempted creation, alteration, or eradication of particular ideas, beliefs, or cultural norms through an intentional campaign of introducing memes designed to achieve the desired objective.

I don't know how many people actually use the phrase "memetic engineering" to describe what they do, but the fact that it is widely—and increasingly—practiced in contemporary society is abundantly evident. And social media is the perfect means of carrying it out. No other tool in history has allowed influencers to reach so many people at once with an idea, or to so quickly and effectively enlist others in spreading the message, as social media does.

Two examples drive this point home. The first is fictional. The most recent thriller from *New York Times* Bestselling author Daniel Suarez is *Kill Decision*, published in 2012. One of the book's plots centers around "sock puppetry" in social media. This is the phenomenon of shadowy organizations using thousands or even millions of fake social media accounts to create the false impression of public support behind any given subject. (On a smaller scale, this occurs all the time on commercial websites, where it's called "astroturfing," or fake grass-roots marketing.) In *Kill Decision*, shadowy intelligence operatives working for corporate and governmental employers use these sock puppet armies to perform "Influence Operations"–staged actions designed to rally and shape public opinion on a given topic. I interviewed Mr. Suarez on this subject for my blog. He concedes that this is not yet a widespread problem online, but says the technology for doing so is so cheap and readily available that it is about to become a major phenomenon. "If a person or organization isn't troubled by ethics, and they want to quickly influence public opinion," he said, "then they're going to create armies of fictitious followers. It's just too easy in an open, anonymous system like today's Internet."

The second example is very much real. In 1996, both houses of Congress easily passed the Defense of Marriage Act, or DOMA. This legislation codified a concept that had been taken for granted in virtually every society on earth for all of human history—that the institution of "marriage" referred to relationships between men and women. Yet in 2013, only 17 years later, many of the same legislators who passed the law, and the former president who signed it, cheered as the Supreme Court ruled it an unconstitutional discrimination against same-sex couples. Regardless of where one stands on this issue, nearly everyone now agrees that it is only a short amount of time before gay marriage is proclaimed to be a fundamental right nationwide, as it has already become in many other countries around the world.

Social scientists and political observers of all stripes were amazed at the rapid pace at which this shift in public opinion took place. When DOMA was adopted, the vast majority of Americans supported it. In subsequent years, dozens of states passed their own versions of the law aimed at prohibiting same-sex marriage. Only a few years before the Court's ruling, that view still commanded majority support in nationwide polls. Today, however, polls reveal an opposite opinion—and you'll be increasingly hard-pressed to find someone willing to publicly oppose same-sex unions. That's because to do so is now a sure-fire way to be immediately branded as an ignorant, hateful, narrow-minded bigot. The viciousness of the rhetoric on this issue is astounding, even by the thick-skinned standard of American politics.

Social media can't get all the credit for this rapid shift in public opinion, but I think it's safe to say that views would not have turned around nearly as quickly as they did without the influence of conversations that took place on Facebook and Twitter. These platforms allow views on hot-button issues—topics that some might find too awkward to raise in person—to be exchanged on the same even playing field as any other idea. Once a controversial view is repeated often enough, it becomes less shocking and more mainstream. And when enough of our friends repeat or espouse the idea, we are less likely to challenge it and more likely to adopt it, as C. S. Lewis observed in the passage quoted above.

The power of social media to champion the particular concept of same-sex marriage came out in full force a few months before the DOMA ruling. The Human Rights Campaign introduced a red version of its logo (an "equals" sign, symbolizing "marriage equality") and encouraged social media users to adopt it as their profile picture. Millions did so, on Facebook, Twitter, Google+ and elsewhere. Even as of this writing, in the summer of 2013, several people are still using it. The effect was hard to overestimate. When a substantial percentage of one's friends adopt the same symbol, the message it conveys becomes impossible to ignore. One can quickly develop the impression that it must be the view held by the majority of the people we trust the most. And that, of course, was exactly the point.

These observations on the power of social media hold true regardless of which view you hold on this or any other specific topic. It is the same truth about the power of friendships demonstrated by C. S. Lewis and Facebook social advertising, applied to the spread of ideas on a societal level. And it is an awesome power indeed. In this context, obeying the warning to "guard your heart" requires more attention and vigilance than ever before.

Don't
miss the
forest for
the trees

Driven to distraction

Fans have repeatedly voted "The Best of Both Worlds" as their favorite episode of the long-running series *Star Trek: The Next Generation*. In it, humanity has its first major encounter with the Borg, a relentless cybernetic race intent on assimilating every other species into their collective. The episode's climactic scene occurs just as a Borg vessel is about to begin assimilating the inhabitants of Earth. Despite gaining access to the enemy ship's internal operating systems, the U.S.S. Enterprise's Commander Data could not manage to hack his way into the Borg's weapons, propulsion, or any other system that might neutralize the imminent threat.

Just when the attack is about to begin, however, the Borg ship goes quiet. All of its mechanistic occupants power down. To his stunned companions, Data explains that he finally thought to access the Borg's "regeneration subroutines," which were not nearly as protected as the systems directly related to combat. "In effect," he says, "I put them all to sleep."

A similar incident occurs in C. S. Lewis' masterpiece *The Screwtape Letters*, a story about the perpetual battle between good and evil from the perspective of one of Satan's minions. Over the course of the book, Lewis uses this literary device to explore all of the negative influences, ideas and thought patterns that prevent us from gaining a better knowledge of God. But one of the first lessons the title character gives his young apprentice is the utility of simple distraction. Screwtape recounts an incident in which his human subject's train of thought was only seconds away from conceding God's sovereignty. Rather than responding with counterarguments, the demon "struck instantly at the part of the man which I had best under my control, and suggested that it was just about time he had some lunch." By the time the man reached the street, his attention had been captured by the hustle and bustle outside, and his thoughts never again strayed so close to the things of God.

Both of these illustrations capture one of the greatest spiritual dangers that social media sites pose to their users. Of course the content we encounter on these sites has the potential to cause us direct spiritual harm. But in many cases, the indirect effect of distraction is just as consequential. By constantly providing new streams of data tailored to our personal interests and inclinations, social media can become an enormous time-suck, distracting us from more meaningful activity and effectively putting our souls to sleep.

Is that assertion a bit dramatic? Perhaps. But for many of us it's right on the mark, exactly because we pay far too little attention to the supernatural drama in which we all play a part. The Bible tells us that God created humanity so that they may enjoy communion with Him, but that we rebelled and let our attention drift away from Him. It also reveals that God is so discontented with this state of affairs that He has sent prophets, performed miracles, and even took human form and died for us, all to win back our love, faith and obedience. But before He can win our devotion, He first has to get our *attention*.

Nor is God satisfied with our occasional affirmations or church attendance. He wants all of us, all the time, to constantly become more like Him. The earliest Scriptures, written nearly four millennia ago, implore us to walk further along the "path" of "wisdom"—Godly living—every moment of our lives. "Obey my commands and live!," shouts Proverbs

7:2-4; "Guard my instructions as you guard your own eyes. Tie them on your fingers as a reminder. Write them deep within your heart." Many centuries later, Paul wrote in 2 Corinthians 10:5 (NIV) that we should strive to "take captive every thought and make it obedient to Christ." These are all calls to a life-long endeavor.

But Jesus warned us that many of those who hear and accept this message will nevertheless become useless to his kingdom *because they will be too distracted* by the things of this world. For these people, he says in Mark 4:19 (ESV), "the cares of this world and the deceitfulness of riches and the desire for other things enter in and choke the word [of God], and it proves unfruitful." I'm willing to bet that every single person reading these words can relate to being distracted from the things of God by "the cares of this world"—and that for many, too much time spent online is a major culprit. I know it's true for me. This book, for example, would have been written months earlier if it weren't for the hours I chose to play *Words With Friends* or scroll through my Facebook newsfeed instead of writing.

What's more, when we examine this phenomenon of distraction in the context of a

Biblical worldview, we see that it's no accident. There is a very literal war raging over our attention span and our desires. In the same parable in which Jesus described distracted believers as plants choked by the weeds of distraction, he noted that "as soon as [some people] hear [the word of God], Satan comes and takes away the word that was sown in them." (Mark 4:13, NIV.) Likewise, 1 Peter 5:8 warns: "Watch out for your great enemy, the devil. He prowls around like a roaring lion, looking for someone to devour." Dark, spiritual forces—much like Lewis' Screwtape—are actively, consciously seeking to lead us astray.

My point is not to label social media as "demonic." Rather, it is to remind us all to be better stewards of our time. "Awake, O sleeper," Paul implores in Ephesians 5:14 (ESV). He continues in verse 15 (ESV): "Look carefully then how you walk, not as unwise but as wise, *making the best use of the time*, because the days are evil." Social media is now the single most popular activity on the internet, and it is constantly migrating onto new platforms and seeping into more of our waking hours. For many of us, therefore, it is one of the likeliest obstacles to "making the best use of the time," if we allow it to be.

Permanent puberty of the mind

Hand-in-hand with the danger of distraction comes the threat of losing the capacity for deep thinking altogether. Our muscles and joints lose range of movement when we don't stretch them far enough or often enough. Something similar happens when we refuse to stretch our minds. And I believe that overconsumption of social media can contribute to this result.

One of my favorite quotes comes from Thomas Traherne, a 17th-Century English poet and theologian. He said: "As nothing is more easy than to think, so nothing is more difficult than to think well." The first half of this quote echoes Rene Descartes' maxim, "I think, therefore I am." Using our minds is the one irreducible complexity that makes us human. We don't pull the plug on a severely injured person, for example, unless they are first declared "brain-dead." Stephen Hawking's body is almost entirely useless, but his active mind keeps him not only human, but in the forefront of modern cosmology.

The ease with which thoughts enter our minds, however, is exactly what makes thinking such a difficult process to discipline. The best we can do is to train our attention on the thought processes we want to cultivate, and try to ignore the ones we don't. So many mental illnesses, bad habits and poor decisions can be traced back to our failure or inability to avoid dwelling on unhealthy thoughts.

It's harder to discern what's worth thinking about and to spend time focusing on it, however, when we're overloaded with a constantly changing variety of inputs. The great blessing of this post-industrial age is the wealth of information at our fingertips. Five-year-olds with iPads blithely skim through more data than the kings of old, with their vast libraries and armies of wise men, could have dreamed of obtaining. Every day, the 24-hour news cycle broadcasts more information than we could possibly consume. Over an hour of video is uploaded to YouTube every second. And between our hundreds of connections on Facebook and Twitter, the conversation never stops.

But as the philosopher Nassim Nicholas Taleb observes in his 2012 book *Antifragile*, "the more frequently you look at data, the more noise [*i.e.,* useless data] you are disproportionately likely to get." News providers need to find *something* to fill all that time, meaning that an increasingly high percentage of the content they publish is more "filler" than "news."

What's more, this "filler"—which mostly consists of what Taleb calls "the anecdote"—becomes so commonplace that we start to think of *that* as being what is significant or newsworthy. A case in point: as I write these words, media outlets are tripping over themselves to outdo each other in covering the birth of England's Prince George Alexander Louis. The comments in my Facebook and Twitter streams are blowing up about it. But could there possibly be anything *less* significant (other than for the Royal Family themselves) to be talking about?

Proverbs 10:19 (NIV) summed this up succinctly: "When words are many, sin is not absent." Social media magnifies this truth. As I've observed, social sites constantly encourage their users to share content, so that the service providers can keep building databases to sell to advertisers. But let's face it—we don't have that much worth saying. Sharing and socializing online can be healthy and edifying up to a point, but we reach a point of diminishing returns much more quickly than we often realize.

The more accustomed we grow to consuming constantly updated streams of information, the less inclined we are to stop looking for more new input and instead dwell on what we've already taken in. A "permanent puberty of the mind" is what Shane Hipps—an advertising strategist, Mennonite pastor, and author of *Flickering Pixels: How Technology Shapes Your Faith*—called this condition in a 2009 interview with *Christianity Today*.[5] He continued:

> "We get locked in so much information, and the inability to sort that information meaningfully limits our capacity to understand. The last stage of knowledge is wisdom. But we are miles from wisdom because the Internet encourages the opposite of what creates wisdom— stillness, time, and inefficient things like suffering. On the Internet, there is no such thing as waiting; there is no such thing as stillness. There is a constant churning."

In the four years since Hipps made that observation, social media has only multiplied our "constant churning" of online information, and occupied even more of the time that we might have otherwise spent processing, thinking, or reflecting on what we've already learned. As a result, the depth of our thoughts—and ultimately, our capacity to *have* deep thoughts—has suffered.

The solution to this problem is to unplug on a regular basis. Limit the amount of time you spend "socializing" with digital friends, skimming news feeds or refreshing your Pinterest screen. Fight against the urge—which I struggle with as much as anyone does—to fill every empty moment with your mobile device. Put it down, take a walk, or just stare out the window for a while, and *think*. As Proverbs 14:8 (NIV) advises, "the wisdom of the prudent is to give thought to their ways." Take stock of where your life is and where it's going.

Better yet, develop the habit of regular solitude and prayer that Jesus modeled for us. People came to him in person rather than online, but he had at least as many "followers" as any of us do on Twitter.[6] He could easily have spent every waking moment healing the sick and teaching the crowds that hung on his every word. But despite how valuable that ministry was, Jesus often got away on his own, and spent his time praying. As C. S. Lewis said, prayer "doesn't change God—it changes me." That time alone with God disciplines our thoughts and refocuses our attention back on the source of all truth and goodness, and equips us to be the person we ought to be when we re-enter the world around us.

Don't be a stumbling block

"What we do in life echoes in eternity."

Russell Crowe's character, General Maximus Decimus Meridius, shouted these words to the soldiers under his command as an encouragement to fight bravely. We Christians are also soldiers, in a manner of speaking. Paul wrote in Ephesians 6:12 (ESV) that we "wrestle against ... the cosmic powers over this present darkness, against the spiritual forces of evil in the heavenly places." The results of our efforts are marked in our own spirits, and in the souls of those we influence in life—which are the only aspects of creation that will continue to exist for all eternity.

Other Christians

In 1 Corinthians 8, Paul exhorted Christians to be mindful of the effect their behavior had on other believers around them. He used the example of meat that had been sacrificed to idols. Many of those who had recently come to faith in Christ had previously considered eating such meat to be a way of worshipping those idols, and for that reason now felt uncomfortable partaking. Faith in Christ brings freedom from such worries, because "we all know that an idol is not really a god and that there is only one God," as Paul said in 1 Corinthians 8:4. But in verse 7 of the same chapter, he noted that some of the more recent converts were still "accustomed to thinking of idols as being real, so when they eat food that has been offered to idols, they think of it as the worship of real gods, and their weak consciences are violated." Therefore, in verses 9-13, Paul warned "stronger" Christians to refrain from eating the meat—not for its own sake, but for the sake of those around them:

> [Y]ou must be careful so that your freedom does not cause others with a weaker conscience to stumble. For if others see you—with your "superior knowledge"—eating in the temple of an idol, won't they be encouraged to violate their conscience by eating food that has been offered to an idol? So because of your superior knowledge, a weak believer for whom Christ died will be destroyed. And when you sin against other believers by encouraging them to do something they believe is wrong, you are sinning against Christ. So if what I eat causes another believer to sin, I will never eat meat again

as long as I live—for I don't want to cause another believer to stumble.

In Christian circles, this has become known as the "weaker brother principle," and has (rightly) been applied to all sorts of circumstances. It need not relate to food, for example, and it doesn't necessarily mean that the other person is "weaker" than you. Rather, the principle is one of considerate self-restraint. If Paul were alive today, he might've written that he would rather delete all of his social media accounts than to post a status update that caused another believer to stumble in his faith.

What sort of situations might this principle apply to in the context of social media? Think of things that some Christians feel free to do, but that others are troubled by. Alcohol is one such issue that I've encountered. I grew up in a community that treated all drinking as sin. As an adult, I re-read the Scriptures and decided that they prohibited only drunkenness, not alcohol in general. So I got in the habit of drinking socially.

It wasn't long, though, before I encountered not only people who considered all drinking wrong, but also those who were recovering (and sometimes, not-so-recovering) alcoholics. I wish I could say that

I never drank in front of such people. I shouldn't have. And today—especially since I'm now a leader within my church community—not only should I avoid drinking in front of those who struggle with alcohol, but I should not be posting photos and updates associating me with alcohol on my social media accounts, either. Not because I'm pretending that I never touch the stuff, but rather because I don't want to be a stumbling block to another believer who struggles with the issue. Even if the context from which such social media content originates is innocent, I simply don't have enough control over who sees it or how it's interpreted. And this wisdom is not limited to the Christian realm; I have spoken with political leaders who avoid posing for pictures with a glass in their hand, for similar reasons.

These are more than hypothetical concerns. I know more than one believer who became disenchanted with church life because of what they saw other Christians doing through social media—both the faults these Christians revealed as well as the perceived hypocrisy of only posting peppy or boastful messages about the good things they enjoyed. I've seen a parent become upset at a church when a children's ministry leader posted photos of that person's child without asking first. More recently, I encountered Christians who were becoming confused, and being led to question some core Biblical doctrines, because a fellow church member had been repeatedly sharing content online that had a feel-good message but that contradicted some basic teachings of Scripture.

Some of these reactions were fair, and some, I thought, were not. But Paul tells us that doesn't matter. We should err on the side of caution, because the consequence of turning a fellow believer away from the church community, or even from the faith, is far worse than anything we stand to gain by sharing the information.

I used a similar cost-benefit analysis not long ago with regard to my social check-ins. I enjoy "checking in" on Yelp!, Foursquare, or Facebook to the restaurants, attractions, and other interesting places I visit. Call me silly (and some do), but I find they're great conversation starters. After all, these are exactly the types of activities you discuss with your friends when you talk to them in person. I especially enjoy checking in when I'm traveling alone on business trips. Not only are the places I'm visiting generally more interesting than my usual routine, but it's also a way to make the experience a little less lonely.

The problem with these out-of-town check-ins, however, was that they made my wife uncomfortable. In her eyes, each such post was a reminder to the rest of the world that she was home alone with two little kids. And after several mutual Facebook friends made innocent comments to her about my travels, she asked me to stop.

This was hard for me at first. It wasn't something I wanted to stop doing, and I marshaled all sorts of arguments in my head about why it shouldn't bother her. But for once, I wisely kept those arguments to myself, and decided to respect her feelings on the subject. I know instinctively that I would lay down my life for my family; it should not have been so difficult to lay down my cell phone for them too.

Everyone Else

Here's a piece of advice that I need to be reminded of as often as anyone else does: we should always talk to people like we want them to come to heaven with us.

This does not mean that we need to be preachy or saccharine. We don't have to restrict our status updates to Bible verses. But it does mean that we should demonstrate love in everything we do and

say. That begins—especially in social media—with our vocabulary. "Avoid all perverse talk; stay away from corrupt speech," says Proverbs 4:24. Likewise, Paul says in Ephesians 5:4 (ESV), "[l]et there be no filthiness nor foolish talk nor crude joking [among you], but instead let there be thanksgiving." I feel a pang of regret every time I read these verses, because I remember how foolish and crude my words have been at times. But that feeling is coupled with relief that at least we didn't have social media when I was in school. I pity the teenagers growing up today while sharing every one of their immature, soon-to-be regretted whims online, where they will be stored, duplicated and accessible for the rest of their lives.

Jesus said in John 13:35 (ESV): "By this all people will know that you are my disciples, if you have love for one another." And in 1 Corinthians 13:1, Paul reiterated: "If I could speak all the languages of earth and of angels, but didn't love others, I would only be a noisy gong or a clanging cymbal." Is love evident in what we're saying online? And if it isn't, what are we accomplishing for God's kingdom?

Brennan Manning said it best:

> The greatest single cause of atheism in the world today is Christians who acknowledge Jesus with their lips and walk out the door and deny Him by their lifestyle. That is what an unbelieving world simply finds unbelievable.

I've shared this well-worn quote in the past, and been attacked for likening atheism to a disease that Christians can either cause or prevent. But an in-depth study[7] published in the June 2013 issue of *The Atlantic* magazine added credence to Manning's insight. The authors interviewed scores of atheist students across the country, and found that, for the vast majority of them:

- They had attended church;
- The mission and message of their churches were vague;
- They felt their churches offered superficial answers to life's difficult questions;
- They expressed respect for those ministers who took the Bible seriously;
- The decision to embrace unbelief was often an emotional one; and
- The internet factored heavily into their conversion to atheism.

Taking these findings together—especially the final one—spells out an ominous warning to Christians about our online behavior: the attitude we demonstrate to others in social media matters. Others, both inside and outside the faith, are looking to you as a representative of Christ's kingdom. And if what they see in your posts doesn't line up with the love that our Scriptures say so much about, there's a real chance that you could be helping to push them away from God altogether.

Be a peacemaker

Vote for Jesus

There are many words one could choose to characterize the tone of most political conversation in America today. But "civil" is not one of them. In fairness, of course, history doesn't give us any indication that political debate has ever been a very agreeable process, in this or any other country. Government affects our lives in ways that hit us where we live, and that can get people riled up at times.

But in today's culture, political warfare has become its own industry, and its intensity rivals that of actual combat. Fueled by talk radio, openly partisan news channels, and demagogue authors from both ends of the political spectrum, there is very little room remaining in the public square for anyone not espousing one extreme or another. And instead of using intellect and reason to appeal to audiences, the talking heads battle for viewers by competing to see whose rhetoric can be more smug, caustic and entertaining.

Moreover, no other era has had the tools available to conduct political warfare on such a massive scale as we do. It was one thing in the past to attend political rallies, post yard signs, and have impassioned arguments with our neighbors. It's another entirely to give, through social media, every single person in the country a platform on which to debate—or, more often, tear down—anyone else in the country who thinks differently than they do.

This attitude has infected the church like a plague. Sometimes, I think, believers are even more prone than others to take political badgering too far. After all, we're accustomed to knowing with all of our heart and soul that a particular set of propositions—*i.e.*, that the Bible is God's Word, that Jesus is the Son of God, and that He died to reconcile us to His Father— is true, and that any claim to the contrary is false. Our commitment to the absolute truth of those beliefs is the very thing that defines us as a community.

The trouble comes when we expand that "blessed assurance" (as an old hymn calls it) to include beliefs that are less certain and not necessary to our faith in Christ. In other words, just because we believe in *an* absolute truth doesn't mean that every single thing you or I believe is absolutely true. When we treat our own particular *interpretations* of Scripture, and even our political views, as Holy Writ, we not only cause harm, but we do it in God's name.

And what harm we cause. In just the short amount of time since the 2008 presidential election campaign began, for example, I have personally witnessed several relationships damaged or broken, and dozens of individuals emotionally wounded, within multiple churches—all because Christians couldn't restrain themselves from attacking the political leanings of other believers on Facebook.

I've spent my life in church, and I've seen certain believers do some pretty appalling things over the years. But some of the things I've seen done online in the name of politics ranks right up there with the worst of it. Several people I know by name, and probably many more that I never did, left their churches—or church life altogether—because of how others in the church conducted their politics online. Rarely in my experience had church looked *less* like a place of love than in these situations.

This should not be. Part of the problem is rooted in the modern proverb, "all's fair in love and war." It means that in these situations, the ends justify the means, and that we're often willing to sacrifice the ethics that might otherwise restrain us from taking certain actions. Applying that mentality to politics—the portion of our lives dedicated to both debating and collaborating with our friends and neighbors to ultimately enhance our common good—can only backfire, both politically and spiritually. We end up trampling on the very lives we're trying to improve.

One of the ethics we jettison when we as Christians apply a wartime mentality to our politics is the one taught by Ephesians 4: 31-32:

> Get rid of all bitterness, rage, anger, harsh words, and slander, as well as all types of evil behavior. Instead, be kind to each other, tenderhearted, forgiving one another, just as God through Christ has forgiven you.

In other words, even if your neighbor is dead wrong politically—so what? Forgive them for that "fault," and treat them tenderly instead of with bitterness.

This is all the more true when we consider that political arguments are never entirely inerrant for all time. As Proverbs 18:17 (NIV) says, "The first to state his case seems right, till another comes forward and questions him." The Bible simply does not take a position on the right to bear arms, universal health insurance, or the appropriate tax rate. You can have positions on these issues and others—even strong opinions—and still retain the humility to acknowledge that another opinion might be valid, or possibly better, and that we remain bonded together in Christian love despite our differences. Even on issues where political and moral beliefs appropriately overlap, we can pursue our view of justice without damaging those who don't see it our way.

In the end, this issue comes down to citizenship. As citizens of the United States, we should respect the democratic process and integrity of our fellow Americans. And as citizens of God's kingdom—which should be our primary allegiance—we are commanded to respect the civil authorities in place, even when we disagree with them. 1 Peter 2:13-17 (ESV) tells us to "honor everyone," including those in power over us. Proverbs 24:21 (NIV) echoes this advice, and warns us, "do not join with rebellious officials" against those in authority. Jesus himself told us in Matthew 22:21 (NIV) to "give back to Caesar what is Caesar's," and in Romans 13:7 (NIV), Paul adds, "if you owe taxes, pay taxes."

Above all, we should value the spiritual condition

of those around us far more than any earthly political agenda.

Take It Offline

Of course, our arguments with each other are not limited to political disputes. Conflict seems to be an integral part of the human experience—and also, therefore, an unavoidable aspect of social media.

The Bible is replete with advice for resolving interpersonal conflict. Jesus spelled out a basic framework for handling disputes between Christians in Matthew 18:15-17:

> If another believer sins against you, go privately and point out the offense. If the other person listens and confesses it, you have won that person back. But if you are unsuccessful, take one or two others with you and go back again, so that everything you say may be confirmed by two or three witnesses. If the person still refuses to listen, take your case to the church. Then if he or she won't accept the church's decision, treat that person as a pagan or a corrupt tax collector.

Notice that the first step is to approach the offending person privately. One on one. Only if that fails does anyone else need to get involved, and even then only "one or two others." It is not appropriate to make the dispute anyone else's business unless both of these initial steps fail.

These principles are not limited to disputes between believers. Proverbs 17:09 (NIV) tells us that a person "who would foster love covers over an offense, but whoever repeats the matter separates close friends." In two other verses—12:16 and 19:11— Proverbs reiterates that a wise person will "overlook" an insult or offense. That is because "the wisdom from above is first pure, then peaceable, gentle, open to reason, full of mercy and good fruits, impartial and sincere," according to James 3:17 (ESV). And Jesus said in Matthew 5:9 (ESV), "Blessed are the peacemakers, for they shall be called the sons of God." At a very fundamental level, living as God intended means reducing conflict and seeking peace.

How completely backwards, then, is our typical approach to social media! Facebook and Twitter seem to have become the *first* resort for airing our grievances. It's as if we do not feel vindicated unless as many people as possible are aware of our troubles. As Todd Wasserman of the news site *Mashable* observed, "Constant access to social media has done some weird things to humanity. Our narcissism is off the charts, and with that comes a penchant for portraying ourselves as public crusaders. Civility, meanwhile, has gone by the wayside."[8] He then collected several examples from just the very recent news of people who made social media their first resort for expressing irritation with someone else.

Another recent study confirmed that anger is the most influential emotion in online interactions. Even when our privacy settings allow less than the entire world to listen in, it is usually no fewer than hundreds of online "friends" that have access to our rants. "Amplify that to thousands of second and third-hand connections, and huge numbers of people can be profoundly affected by seemingly innocent keystrokes."[9] Take a look at your Facebook news feed; how often is someone's complaint *not* within the first ten results?

This phenomenon is so endemic across our society that social media has become a routine resource for evidence in court. This is especially true in family courts. Divorce and custody battles are the types of disputes that affect us most deeply on an emotional level, so if we're already prone to airing our grievances online, our feelings about such matters are likely to end up there as well. But in countless cases, such online rants have backfired by causing a court to question the person's emotional fitness as a parent or their good faith toward their spouse. Not long ago, a nearby women's shelter consulted me in the course of drafting a social media policy for their residents. Because so many of their clients had shot themselves in the foot this way online, the shelter particularly needed help driving this point home to them. Therefore, the policy I drafted for them did not mince words. It said: "DO NOT RANT about your ex-partner. Ever. Seriously. Facebook is not your support group." A little harsh, perhaps. But necessary.

Even when our goal is to *resolve* conflict, we're doing it wrong if a post on our Facebook walls is our first resort. Indeed, it's hard to imagine a situation where plastering our interpersonal grievances online for the world to see is ever truly appropriate from a Biblical perspective. Wasserman reached the same conclusion from a secular viewpoint as well. He wrote: "The next time you feel outraged about something someone near you is doing, put your phone down and go talk to that person. Either that or shut up and mind your own business."

I have had plenty of opportunity to put these principles into practice—sometimes regarding things that happened offline, and also regarding insults inflicted through social media itself. If there is one piece of advice we should remember in these situations, it's this: *take it offline.* At a minimum, if someone insults you on your Facebook wall, respond with a private Facebook message rather than a public comment. Even better, though, is picking up the phone or speaking to the person face-to-face. Whether it's public or private, written correspondence lacks the expression, emotion and tone that makes up so much of human communication. These elements are often crucial to conveying your intent accurately and avoiding unintended offense. We even see this truth expressed in 2 Corinthians 10:1, where Paul acknowledges, "I realize you think I am timid in person and bold only when I write from far away."

These same principles apply when other people's complaints show up in our news feeds. We can be just as guilty of "repeating a matter," as Proverbs 17:9 says, and fanning the flames of conflict when we talk about problems that other people have shared online. Indeed, Proverbs uses a very familiar word to describe this activity—"gossip"—and has a lot to say against it. In verses 16:28 and 25:23, Proverbs tells us that gossiping destroys friendships. And "interfering in someone else's argument," says Proverbs 26:17, "is as foolish as yanking a dog's ears."

Eliminating this source of conflict is easy: "Fire goes out without wood, and quarrels disappear when gossip stops," according to Proverbs 26:20. The trouble is that gossip is just so tempting. Some basic element of human nature gives us an overwhelming urge to concern ourselves with other people's private business. Twice, in verses 18:8 and 26:22 (NIV), Proverbs acknowledges that "the words of a gossip are like choice morsels; they go down to the inmost parts."

That's why it can be so hard to avoid repeating what we hear about others. Social media—the entire purpose of which is to broadcast the details of our lives—certainly doesn't make this easy. But resisting the temptation is worth the struggle.

Build *genuine* community

What is a friend?

In the Summer of 2008, Toronto-based author Hal Niedzviecki was feeling lonely. Like many of us in mid-life, he found that work obligations and family commitments had left him feeling socially isolated. But online, he was a superstar, with almost 700 Facebook friends. So he performed an experiment. He invited every one of those friends to a party. Of the 700, 15 committed to attending, while 60 said maybe. Satisfied even with that minimal degree of feedback, Hal got dressed up and went out to the local pub, excited for an evening of conversation.

But no one showed up—except for one woman he hardly knew who arrived late, then quickly excused herself when she found out she was the only guest. So Hal spent the night on a bar stool, promising himself he'd spend less time online going forward. "Seven hundred friends," he wrote in a *New York Times* piece a few months later, "and I was drinking alone."[10]

Like Hal, it's easy for us to fall for the illusion that we are being social merely because we consume "social media." For one thing, much of the "socializing" we do online is asynchronous; I'll read a status update that a friend may have posted hours earlier, and maybe add a comment to a thread that others contribute to for days, but we're not really *conversing* with each other. That level of interaction is more akin to throwing message-bearing bottles into the sea and hoping we get one back someday.

Even when we chat with each other online in real time, there's a level of intimacy that's missing. For the same reason we feel more comfortable "flaming" others or using sharper language in print than we would in person, so too do we get less gratification even from pleasant words posted online.

This is not to say that online interactions have no socially redeeming value. But in order to get value from them, we need to be mindful of the medium's limitations, and tailor our expectations accordingly.

Regardless of the medium, if we're going to build strong friendships with others, we first have to understand what a "friend" really is. The Book of Proverbs has a lot to say about friendship. The quality of a good friend that it stresses more than any other is *loyalty*. Proverbs 17:17, 18:24, and 20:6 reiterate that "a friend is always loyal." Verse 27:10 instructs: "Never abandon a friend." Likewise, verse 3:3 says, "Never let loyalty and kindness leave you."

I confess to having been surprised by this at first. I had expected the primary focus to be something more spiritual, such as the importance of a friend who fears God.

But the more I thought about it, the more it made sense. We interact in passing with hundreds of people during the course of an average day, with more and more of these fleeting "relationships" occurring entirely online. A friend stands out from this crowd by investing themselves in our lives, and being someone on whom we can rely. This is a fundamental quality of what it means to be a friend. We have a phrase for people who claim to be our friends, yet prove unreliable when we really need them: "fair weather friend." By contrast, a true friend remains devoted, uncompromising, reliable—loyal—to us, no matter the circumstances.

Knowing that a friend is loyal to you means being able to trust that their advice is given with your best interests in mind. In the midst of a world that so often tears us down, that kind of sincerity can mean more to us than the advice itself. As Proverbs 27:9

says, "The heartfelt counsel of a friend is as sweet as perfume and incense."

This does not mean, of course, that what our friend says will be easy to hear. Consider this well-known passage in Proverbs 27:17: "As iron sharpens iron, so a friend sharpens a friend." How do two pieces of iron sharpen each other? By colliding into and scraping against each other, sending sparks flying. We do our friends and ourselves a disservice if we expect all our conversations to be hugs and happiness. Sometimes we *need* our friends to speak uncomfortable but necessary words into our lives, because they are the only ones who know us well enough to know that we need to hear them, and the only ones we trust enough to hear those words from.

A relational tool

Social media offers us plenty of ways to be *that* kind of friend. At the very least, fleeting interactions online help maintain a baseline relationship with people we'd otherwise have no contact with at all. There are so many people whose company I have treasured at one point in my life or another, but that I'd lost touch with until we rediscovered each other on Facebook. More often than not, the "rekindled" friendship doesn't extend beyond the exchange of a couple fond messages. But at least now we can find each other if we need to, and I have some idea of what's going on in their lives. That is a starting point for deeper interaction in the future, if nothing else.

For those we see in person, moreover, social media can be a springboard into more personal conversation. Instead of, "Hi, how are you?" your greeting can be, "Hey, I saw the pictures you posted from your camping trip last week. That looked like fun!" This demonstrates to your friend that you've been thinking about them.

But social media also provides plenty of opportunities to demonstrate loyalty. People increasingly turn to Facebook and Twitter to bare their souls and vent their frustrations. How we react is one measure of our loyalty to that friend. Do we treat it as another awkward, perhaps even irritating bit of data in our news feeds? Or do we pause to consider how our friend is feeling, and offer encouragement? It might be a comment, a private message, or even pausing to whisper a prayer on that friend's behalf. If we skim over the uncomfortable updates in search of more entertaining fare, however, we've demonstrated a lack of loyalty to that friend.

On one particular occasion not long ago, I was doing the exact thing that I've criticized so often—pulling out my phone to fill a few empty seconds in a restaurant by skimming Facebook. But that's when I read a heart-felt admission of grief from someone who'd just received a grim medical diagnosis. And although this was someone I knew from church, I'd never had much opportunity to really get to know him. It would have been easy to sigh, feel bad for a second, and keep skimming.

But I felt an immediate tug on my spirit not to be so callous. As it happened, I was part of a group of leaders participating in a time of prayer that coming Sunday. So rather than clicking "like" or even sending a note of encouragement, I used that point of digital connection to invite that friend to let me pray with him in person. Rarely have I been so clear in knowing I was doing the exact thing that God wanted me to do in a situation. The resulting interactions were deeply meaningful for both of us, and planted the seeds for a genuine friendship that continues to grow.

I am not the only one to have used social media this way. A friend of mine who does youth ministry recently shared with me how thankful he is for his Facebook friendships with the teens in his youth group. These give him and his fellow leaders a window into the problems the teens face. Youth who would never admit a problem to an adult in person often have no hesitation in posting it online. And when they do, one of the youth leaders can respond with a direct message or phone call to offer counsel. Better yet, when the teens know that someone who cares is listening, it can encourage them to seek the comfort of community. I've noticed that the youth in my church have adopted a phrase—"Shake the gates!"—as their way of asking Facebook friends to pray for someone in need.

Of course, almost anything that's good can be taken to an unhealthy extreme, and that's true of loyalty as well. This isn't as obvious of a pitfall in social media, but I see it far too often. As important as it is to be supportive of our friends, we also need to discern when our friends are veering off the reservation, so to speak, and to not support them in doing so. Just days before writing these words, I saw it happen on a church's Facebook page. A pastor used the page to announce his resignation, and to share a few jibes at the church's leaders in the process. Reflexively, a number of his supporters posted words of encouragement, and before anyone knew it, a church split had formed online. Subtler examples occur all the time, such as when someone posts a vague observation or philosophical statement that was intended as an implied jab at someone else. If we aren't careful, a "like" or supportive comment that we intend as merely an encouragement to a friend can be interpreted as taking sides in an argument we didn't even realize was happening.

Iron can also sharpen iron online, when social media puts us in a position to hold our friends accountable. Of course, if our primary approach to social media is as a way to dig up dirt on our friends, we're not likely to maintain many relationships for long enough to do anyone any good. But as we've seen, people sometimes do stupid things online. And when they do, their online "friends" will probably see it. The true *friends* among them will call the person out on their poor choice, if it's a serious enough issue. These are awkward, difficult conversations even in the best of circumstances. But if done with sincerity and love, the friendship—and the friends—will be better for it.

I've had multiple opportunities to deliver a rebuke through social media. At times it was because I'd been offended by what a friend said to me or my loved ones online. In other cases I had noticed that a friend had really crossed the line during an online political spat or by posting an inappropriate photo. And at least once, I stumbled across a friend engaging in conduct that was obviously inconsistent with his marital vows.

The appropriate thing for me to say in each of these situations varied, from a gentle correction to direct confrontation. But in each case, I took my own advice by "taking it offline," either in a private message, phone call, or in-person conversation. Rarely is there anything to gain by adding more fuel to the fire in a public setting. Nearly every one of these encounters ended well, with friendships restored and even strengthened. And I don't regret initiating any of them.

Whatever the circumstances, any interaction we engage in through *social* media should ultimately be geared toward building up other people and strengthening our relationships with them— preferably, relationships that also occur at least partially in person. Hebrews 10:25 instructs, "let us not neglect our meeting together, as some people do, but encourage one another." Social media offers more opportunities to connect with others than humans have ever had before. The ease of online communication makes it more tempting than ever to forego meeting together in person. But there's a reason that sites like Meetup.com and "tweet-up" gatherings are so popular today—because the hunger for genuine community is something we all feel. This verse's reminder, therefore, has never been more needed than it is today. As it suggests, there is encouragement that flows out of in-person community. It is the context in which we were designed to live. Therefore, we should always approach social media as a tool for building genuine, live relationships, not as a substitute for them.

Conclusion

"That's the whole story," as Ecclesiastes 12:13 says. It continues: "Here now is my final conclusion: Fear God and obey his commands, for this is everyone's duty." That summation is equally apt for this book as well. Based on my personal experience and observations while using social media and studying it as both an attorney and as a committed Christ-follower, I organized my thoughts under these seven headers:

1. Think before you post
2. To your own self be true
3. Guard your heart
4. Don't miss the forest for the trees
5. Don't be a stumbling block
6. Be a peacemaker
7. Build genuine community

Hopefully, these seven principles will be helpful reminders to you as you seek to honor God in how you live online, and to apply his wisdom to your interactions in social media. But the principles I chose are arbitrary ways of subdividing and explaining the one basic principle that underlies them all: "Fear God and obey his commands." Or, as Jesus put it in Matthew 22:37-40, quoting another portion of the Old Testament: "Love the Lord your God with all your heart and with all your soul and with all your mind … [and] love your neighbor as yourself."

The technological means that we humans use to interact with each other and to fill our days constantly change with time. Indeed, the social media I discuss in this book may already be at least partially obsolete by the time the book sees print. But God's desire for how we should live our lives does not change. Regardless of what technology we use or circumstances we encounter, let's be discerning of the effect it has on us and on others, and be intentional in using it to live like Jesus told us to.

Endnotes

1. For example, on September 25, 2013, Popular Science announced that it was turning off the comments portion of its website. While not suggesting "that all, or even close to all, of our commenters are shrill, boorish specimens of the lower internet phyla," wrote the magazine's online content director, "even a fractious minority wields enough power to skew a reader's perception of a story." Suzanne LaBarre, "Why We're Shutting Off Our Comments," *Popular Science*, Sept. 24, 2013, available at < http://www.popsci.com/science/article/2013-09/why-were-shutting-our-comments?src=SOC&dom=tw >.

2. Kurt Vonnegut, MOTHER NIGHT (Harpercollins: 1966).

3. Richard Dawkins, "Is Science a Religion?", *The Humanist* 57 (1989), 26-9.

4. Richard Dawkins, THE SELFISH GENE: 30TH ANNIVERSARY EDITION 190-91 (Oxford Univ. Press: 2006).

5. "From the Printing Press to the iPhone," *Christianity Today* (May 6, 2009), available at <http://www.christianitytoday.com/ct/2009/may/20.64.html>.

6. Indeed, Vatican cardinal Gianfranco Ravasi recently went so far as to call Jesus the "world's first tweeter," because his pronouncements were "brief and full of meaning." See "Jesus was 'world's first tweeter', says Vatican cardinal," *The Telegraph*, Sept. 25, 2013, available at < http://www.telegraph.co.uk/news/worldnews/europe/vaticancityandholysee/10334960/Jesus-was-worlds-first-tweeter-says-Vatican-cardinal.html >.

7. Larry Alex Taunton, "Listening to Young Atheists: Lessons for a Stronger Christianity," *The Atlantic* (June 5, 2013), available at < http://www.theatlantic.com/national/archive/2013/06/listening-to-young-atheists-lessons-for-a-stronger-christianity/276584/>.

8. Todd Wasserman, "Social Media-Based Public Shaming Has Gotten Out of Control," Mashable, Mar. 24, 2013, available at < http://mashable.com/2013/03/24/public-shaming-out-of-control/ >.

9. Nick English, "Anger is the Internet's most powerful emotion," *USA Today*, Sept. 24, 2013, available at < http://www.usatoday.com/story/news/nation/2013/09/24/anger-internet-most-powerful-emotion/2863869/ >.

10. "Facebook in a Crowd," *New York Times Magazine* (Oct. 24, 2008), available at <http://www.nytimes.com/2008/10/26/magazine/26lives-t.html?_r=0>.